SATAN'S STRATEGY
TO DESTROY
THE CHURCH

Satan's Strategy to Destroy the Church by Michael Shenton

This book is written to provide information and motivation to readers. Its purpose is not to render any type of psychological, legal, or professional advice of any kind. The content is the sole opinion and expression of the author, and not necessarily that of the publisher.

Copyright © 2025 by Michael Shenton

All rights reserved. No part of this book may be reproduced, transmitted, or distributed in any form by any means, including, but not limited to, recording, photocopying, or taking screenshots of parts of the book, without prior written permission from the author or the publisher. Brief quotations for noncommercial purposes, such as book reviews, permitted by Fair Use of the U.S. Copyright Law, are allowed without written permissions, as long as such quotations do not cause damage to the book's commercial value.

ISBN: 978-1-951670-59-7 (Paperback)
ISBN: 978-1-951670-60-3 (Digital)

Printed in the United States of America.

SATAN'S STRATEGY TO DESTROY THE CHURCH

MICHAEL SHENTON

OTHER CHRISTIAN BOOKS BY MICHAEL SHENTON

- ♦ The Ages of God - A Three-part Series:
- ♦ Book 1. The New Apostolic Age
- ♦ Book 2. The New Holy Spirit Age
- ♦ Book 3. The Temple Veil Torn in Two

For: The New Apostolic Age

Amazon: https://amazon.ca/New-Apostolic-Age-Ages-Book-ebook/dp/B0D5FGCDRN
Booktopia :https://www.booktopia.com.au/the-new-apostolic-age-michael-shenton/ebook/9781951670528.html

Weltbild: https://www.weltbild.de/artikel/ebook/the-new-apostolic-age-the-ages-of-god-bd- 1_43911995-1

Perusall : https://app.perusall.com/catalog/book/4rM5aPnuBp6HNNdvn

Fnac: https://www.fnac.com/livre-numerique/a20615429/Michael-Shenton-The-New-Apostolic-Age#FORMAT=ebook%20(ePub)

FOR: THE NEW HOLY SPIRIT AGE

Amazon: https://www.amazon.ca/Ages-God-II-Holy-Spirit-ebook/dp/B0D5FDQNXC
Booktopia: https://www.booktopia.com.au/the-ages-of-god-ii-the-new-holy-spirit-age-michael- shenton/ebook/9781951670542.html

Weltbild: https://www.weltbild.de/artikel/ebook/the-ages-of-god-ii-the-new-holy-spirit-age-the- ages-of-god_43912074-1

Perusall: https://app.perusall.com/catalog/book/8JqXvy3Tdujwrkq2F

Fnac: https://www.fnac.com/livre-numerique/a20614671/Michael-Shenton-The-Ages-of-God- II-The-New-Holy-Spirit-Age#FORMAT=ebook%20(ePub)

For: The Temple Veil Torn in Two

Amazon: https://www.amazon.ca/Ages-God-III-Temple-Veil-ebook/dp/B0D5FH21PP
Booktopia: https://www.booktopia.com.au/the-ages-of-god-iii-michael- shenton/ebook/9781951670559.html

Weltbild: https://www.weltbild.de/artikel/ebook/the-ages-of-god-iii-the-ages-of-god-bd- 3_43912081-1

Perusall: https://app.perusall.com/catalog/book/5yKFirem6YyZ74HEv

Fnac: https://www.fnac.com/livre-numerique/a20615192/Michael-Shenton-The-Ages-of-God- III#FORMAT=ebook%20 (ePub)

CONTENTS

INTRODUCTION XV

The Keys to Being Used by God................................. xv
The Vision of Jesus.. xix
The Church's Disrespect of Christ xx

CHAPTER 1: THE VISION AND REVELATION 1

The Vision of Jesus..2
The Church's Disrespect of Christ................................3
The Purpose of This Book..3

CHAPTER 2: THE GARDEN OF EDEN 5

Satan's Strategy in the Garden of Eden.......................5
The Consequences of Satan's Strategy..........................8
The Transfer of Sin...9

CHAPTER 3: THE FIRST CHURCH IN JERUSALEM 11

The False Gospel in the Jerusalem Church................ 11
Key Challenges in the First Church........................... 12
The Impact of Jesus' Ministry.................................... 15
The First Major Division.. 16

The Long-Term Consequences *16*
Examples of False Gospel Influence *17*

CHAPTER 4: THE TRUE CHURCH IN ANTIOCH 19

A Spirit-Led Church *19*
Characteristics of the Antioch Church *20*
Satan's Attack on Antioch *21*
The Legacy of Antioch *23*
Conclusion *24*

CHAPTER 5: THE CURRENT CHURCH 25

The Greatest Challenge: Division and Doctrine *26*
Key Problems in the Current Church *26*
Historical Influence *30*
Examples of Modern Failings *30*
A Call to Return to the True Church *31*

CHAPTER 6: THE TRUE GOSPEL 33

The Core Message of the True Gospel *33*
Characteristics of a Gospel-Centered Life *36*
The Gospel in Action *37*
Conclusion *37*

CHAPTER 7: THE FALSE GOSPEL 39

Characteristics of a False Gospel *39*
Examples of False Gospel Teachings *41*
The Danger of False Gospels *42*
The Role of Church Leadership in False Gospels *43*
Recognizing and Rejecting a False Gospel *43*

Conclusion *44*

CHAPTER 8: GOD'S PLAN FOR THE CHURCH 47

The Purpose of the Church *47*
The Structure of the Church *50*
Empowering Every Believer *50*
Challenges to God's Plan *51*
Returning to God's Design *52*
Conclusion *52*

CHAPTER 9: GOD-APPOINTED CHURCH STRUCTURE 55

The Biblical Framework *56*
The Purpose of the Structure *57*
Unity Through Diversity *58*
Challenges to God's Design *58*
Returning to the Biblical Model *59*
Conclusion *60*

CHAPTER 10: INDIVIDUAL CHRISTIANS 63

The Identity of a Christian *63*
The Role of Individual Christians *65*
Challenges Faced by Individual Christians *67*
Overcoming Challenges *68*
Conclusion *69*

CHAPTER 11: PEOPLE APPOINTED BY GOD 71

Characteristics of God-Appointed Individuals *72*
Examples of God-appointed People in Scripture *73*
How to Recognize Someone Appointed by God *74*

Modern-day Appointments *76*
Responding to God's Call *77*
Conclusion *77*

CHAPTER 12: DIVISIONS IN THE CHURCH 79

The Root Causes of Division *80*
Biblical Examples of Division *81*
The Consequences of Division *82*
Steps to Overcome Division *83*
The Power of Unity *85*
Conclusion *85*

CHAPTER 13: SATAN'S STRATEGY AGAINST THE CHURCH 87

Satan's Tactics Against the Church *88*
Historical Examples of Satan's Strategy *90*
Satan's Strategy Today *91*
How to Recognize and Resist Satan's Strategy *92*
Conclusion *94*

CHAPTER 14: OVERCOMING SATAN'S STRATEGY 95

Steps to Overcome Satan's Strategies *95*
The Power of Worship *99*
Spiritual Armor *100*
Conclusion *101*

CHAPTER 15: SPIRITUAL WARFARE 103

The Reality of Spiritual Warfare *104*
Weapons for Spiritual Warfare *105*
The Armor of God *107*

Strategies for Victory... *108*
The Role of the Church in Spiritual Warfare *109*
Conclusion *110*

CHAPTER 18: THE FINAL VICTORY 111

The Promise of Victory... *112*
The Nature of the Final Victory.............................. *113*
Living in the Hope of Victory................................. *115*
Conclusion *117*

ABOUT THE AUTHOR 119

INTRODUCTION

Hello everyone, and welcome. My name is Michael Shenton.

I want to encourage you by saying that you can be useful to advance God's Kingdom. I am not someone special, nor am I greater than you in any way. The main keys to being God's steward are:

- Spending time in God's presence
- Developing a personal relationship with Jesus
- Learning to hear the voice of the Holy Spirit
- Obeying the leading of the Holy Spirit
- Having faith and trust in God
- Being filled with the Holy Spirit and power

The Holy Spirit led me to write this book. In January 2019, while I was on a mine site at

McArthur River Mining, one hour from Darwin, Western Australia, Jesus appeared to me in my room. *(See Chapter 1 for the full description.)*

In summary, Jesus said:

1. The Church is disrespecting me by treating my Crucifixion with contempt as if it were not a big deal.
2. The Church is preaching a false Gospel.
3. Priests and pastors have made themselves intermediaries between the people and me. As a result, the people do not have a direct relationship with me.
4. Priests and pastors are blocking the Holy Spirit from ministering in the Church.
5. The season has changed. Jesus said He would remove priests and pastors who oppose the Holy Spirit and would close down churches that oppose the Holy Spirit.

I have observed that many mainline churches in Perth and Southwest Australia (though not all) are dying. The average age of congregations is between 60–80 years, with hardly any children or teenagers. Many of these churches operate like social clubs, where members meet every Sunday with no intention of obeying God or allowing the Holy Spirit to minister.

This lack of spiritual vitality has led to a significant decline in the Church. Many congregations have no desire to preach the Gospel, heal the sick, cast out demons, or raise the dead.

This problem stems from Satan's strategy to destroy the Church. Unfortunately, Church leaders often fail to recognize this spiritual warfare. When you do not acknowledge that you are at war, your enemy can destroy you while you carry on with your everyday life.

The purpose of this book is to explain Satan's strategy to destroy the Church. It is the same strategy he used:

- To destroy Adam and Eve in the Garden of Eden
- To destroy the first Church in Jerusalem
- To destroy the first Church in Rome

It is the same strategy Satan is using today to destroy countless churches and Christians worldwide.

It is worth noting that some churches and Christians have not fallen for Satan's strategy. However, when a Christian led by the Holy Spirit attends a church operating under Satan's strategy, the leadership often tries to undermine that person and their ministry.

For instance, a woman once stood and delivered a word from God in a church. The pastor deliberately pulled her chair away, causing her to fall to the floor. This act was meant to ridicule her and discredit her ministry within that church. I know personally that this occurred.

The most common tactic used by church leaders to destroy someone's ministry is to claim the individual is "not from God." They spread such accusations to others without addressing the person directly. When the accused attempts to meet with church leadership to resolve the matter, they refuse to meet but continue spreading rumors and lies.

This is one way Satan works to destroy
God's people. I have personally experienced
this, enduring false accusations and
lies about me for over 20 years.

How do we know if someone
is appointed by God?

Jesus said, *"You shall know them by their fruit."*
Paul and Barnabas boldly preached the word of
God, and God confirmed their ministry with
signs and wonders. Paul also said, "I did not
come with wise and persuasive words but with a
demonstration of God's power, so that your faith
may not rest on men's wisdom but on God's power."

God's intention for His appointed
believers is that they should:

- ♦ Preach the Gospel.
- ♦ Heal the sick.
- ♦ Cast out demons.
- ♦ Raise the dead.

If a church leader does not display any
spiritual fruit, we should question whether that
person was appointed by God or by man.

Although many Christians may perform good works and display the fruit of the Holy Spirit, they fall short of the fullness of the victory Jesus won for them on the Cross. As Jesus said, *"He who believes in me will do the works that I do, and even greater works than these shall he do."* We should aim for those greater works.

Satan's greatest strategy to destroy the Church is to prevent Christians from knowing and exercising the authority they have in Christ. He ensures churches block believers from understanding or using their God-given authority.

The false Gospel Satan promotes often includes these lies:

1. This authority passed away with the first apostles.
2. Only priests or pastors have this authority.
3. You are a miserable sinner and cannot possibly have this authority.

The most important thing we can have as Christians is a personal relationship with Jesus. Without Jesus, we can do nothing.

The Holy Spirit is God's representative on earth. His role is to:

- ♠ Make Jesus real to us.
- ♠ Allow Jesus to speak to us. (Jesus said, *"My sheep know my voice."*)
- ♠ Equip us with power and authority from Jesus. (John said, *"Jesus will baptize us with the Holy Spirit and fire."*)

When the Holy Spirit came upon the disciples on the day of Pentecost, they were filled with power and began speaking in other tongues as the Spirit enabled them. This baptism of the Holy Spirit, once exclusive to Jews and Gentiles, can now be transferred through the laying on of hands.

Acts 9:17–18 states:

"And Ananias went his way and entered the house; and laying his hands on him he said, 'Brother Saul, the Lord Jesus, who appeared to you on the road as

you came, has sent me that you may receive your sight and be filled with the Holy Spirit.' Immediately there fell from his eyes something like scales, and he received his sight at once; and he arose and was baptized."

The belief that the laying on of hands ceased with the first apostles is a false Gospel.

CHAPTER 1

The Vision and Revelation

In January 2019, I was working at the McArthur River Mine site, located an hour from Darwin in Western Australia. I was staying at the mine camp.

At around 3:00 a.m., after finishing my shower, I stood at the sink, ready to brush my teeth. Suddenly, I heard a soft "blip" sound and felt two drops of liquid land on my feet. When I looked down, I saw two small drops of red blood—one on each foot.

Confused, I thought, "*This is very strange.*" As I pondered what could be happening,

I heard "blip, blip, blip" and noticed more blood on my feet. Alarmed, I began inspecting myself to see if I was bleeding.

As I checked my body, I suddenly heard louder *"blip, blip, blip"* sounds and saw blood appear out of thin air, landing on my feet. By now, a small but significant pool of blood had formed, and I started to feel fear and confusion.

Then, in an instant, Jesus appeared in the room.

He was wearing a long white robe with a golden sash, His brown hair framing His piercing blue eyes. He stood before me, and His presence was overwhelming.

Jesus spoke to me and said:

1. ***"I am disappointed with My Church. They are disrespecting Me. They are treating My crucifixion with contempt, as if it were not a significant event."***

    He explained, *"Think about how you felt a few minutes ago—confused, afraid, and overwhelmed by what was happening. Now imagine the unimaginable pain, suffering, and trauma I endured during My crucifixion. I was innocent yet wrongly accused. I was spat on, beaten, scourged, crowned with thorns, and nailed through My hands and feet. Hanging from the cross, I experienced excruciating pain, dislocated bones, torn muscles, and struggled to breathe. Despite this, many treat My sacrifice as though it were not a big deal."*

2. ***"The Church is preaching a false Gospel."***
3. ***"Priests and pastors have positioned themselves as intermediaries between the people and Me. They are preventing the people from having a direct relationship with Me."***
4. ***"Priests and pastors are blocking the Holy Spirit from ministering in the Church."***
5. ***"The season has changed."***

> Jesus declared, *"I will remove priests and pastors who oppose the Holy Spirit, and I will close down churches that resist Him."*

Stunned, I asked Jesus what this false Gospel was and what needed to be done to address these issues.

He replied, ***"The Holy Spirit will give you revelation and show you what must be done."***

With those words, Jesus disappeared from the room, leaving me deeply shaken yet resolute. Despite the overwhelming experience, I went to work later that day, carrying the weight of His message.

CHAPTER 2

The Garden of Eden

To understand Satan's strategy against the Church, it is vital to revisit his approach in the Garden of Eden. His tactics remain the same—they were effective then, and they are still being used to destroy churches and individual believers today.

SATAN'S STRATEGY IN THE GARDEN OF EDEN

1. He directs your attention toward something.
2. He gives you a desire for that something.
3. He convinces you that something is good for you.

4. He reminds you or questions what God has said.
5. He contradicts God, saying that what God said is not true.
6. He suggests, *"God only said this because He does not want you to be blessed."*
7. You see that it is good to eat, pleasant to the eyes, and desirable for gaining wisdom.
8. You rebel against God and do what Satan suggests.
9. You lose intimacy with God.
10. You experience spiritual death—separation from God.

Anything that Satan says that opposes God's Word is a false Gospel. A false Gospel is when Satan adds to what God has said, reduces it, or directly contradicts it.

Scriptural Foundation

Let us revisit the Scriptures from Genesis to see how this strategy unfolded:

Genesis 2:15–17

"The Lord God took the man and put him in the Garden of Eden to work it and take care of it. And the Lord God commanded the man, 'You are free to eat from any tree in the garden; but you must not eat from the tree of the knowledge of good and evil, for when you eat from it you will certainly die.'"

Genesis 3:1–7

"Now the serpent was more crafty than any of the wild animals the Lord God had made. He said to the woman, 'Did God really say, "You must not eat from any tree in the garden"?' The woman said to the serpent, 'We may eat fruit from the trees in the garden, but God did say, "You must not eat fruit from the tree that is in the middle of the garden, and you must not touch it, or you will die."' 'You will not certainly die,' the serpent said to the woman. 'For God knows that when you eat from it your eyes will be opened, and you will be like God, knowing good and evil.' When the woman saw that the fruit of the tree was good for food and pleasing to the eye,

and also desirable for gaining wisdom, she took some and ate it. She also gave some to her husband, who was with her, and he ate it.

Then the eyes of both of them were opened, and they realized they were naked; so they sewed fig leaves together and made coverings for themselves."

The Consequences of Satan's Strategy

1. Adam and Eve doubted God's Word, effectively calling Him a liar.
2. They experienced spiritual death—separation from God.
3. God provided them with physical clothing made of skin.
4. They were banished from the Garden of Eden.
5. An angel with a flaming sword guarded the Garden to prevent them from returning.
6. Humanity's spirit was separated from God, resulting in spiritual death for all descendants of Adam.

The Transfer of Sin

Adam's sin was passed down through the male line. The female line did not inherit this sin directly. However, when a man and woman united as one flesh, the woman also bore the consequences of sin.

This is why Jesus had to be conceived by the Holy Spirit in the Virgin Mary. Jesus was born without sin because the sin passed down through the male line was absent in His conception. As a result, Jesus became the perfect, sinless offering to take away the sins of the world.

Hebrews 4:15

"For we do not have a high priest who is unable to empathize with our weaknesses, but we have one who has been tempted in every way, just as we are—yet he did not sin."

CHAPTER 3

The First Church in Jerusalem

Satan's strategy to destroy the first Church in Jerusalem closely mirrors his approach in the Garden of Eden. While the specifics varied, the underlying tactics remained consistent— deception, division, and the introduction of a false Gospel.

THE FALSE GOSPEL IN THE JERUSALEM CHURCH

As Paul highlights in the book of Galatians, a false Gospel plagued the Church in Jerusalem. This Gospel claimed that faith in Jesus Christ was insufficient for salvation and that adherence to the Law of Moses, including circumcision, was necessary.

This issue first arose in Acts 10:44 with the emergence of the "Circumcision Party"—a group that insisted on the necessity of circumcision for salvation:

Acts 11:1–3

"Now the apostles and believers throughout Judea heard that the Gentiles also had received the word of God. So when Peter went up to Jerusalem, the circumcised believers criticized him and said, 'You went into the house of uncircumcised men and ate with them.'"

Key Challenges in the First Church

The following factors contributed to the struggles within the Jerusalem Church:

1. **Jewish Tradition**
    The first converts in Jerusalem were Jews accustomed to worshiping at the Temple. Initially, their meetings

were held there, reinforcing their reliance on the Temple system.

2. **Lack of Authority**
   These converts were used to obeying Temple priests and had little understanding of their spiritual authority as believers.

3. **Converted Temple Priests**
   Some priests who joined the Church sought to maintain their positions of authority and respect.

4. **Legalism**
   These priests were accustomed to administering the Law of Moses and acting as intermediaries between the people and God.

5. **Resistance to Change**
   They struggled to accept that the sacrifices, laws, and traditions of the Old Covenant were no longer required in Christ.

6. **Exclusivity**
   Jewish believers were hesitant to accept Gentiles as equals in the faith.

7. **False Apostles**
   Members of the Circumcision Party, including converted Pharisees, viewed themselves as superior to apostles like Peter, whom they considered unlearned.

8. **Promotion of a False Gospel**
   These individuals preached that salvation required circumcision and obedience to the Mosaic Law, undermining the sufficiency of Christ's sacrifice.

Paul addressed this issue strongly in his letter to the Galatians:

Galatians 1:6–9

"I am astonished that you are so quickly deserting the one who called you to live in the grace of Christ and is turning to a different Gospel—which is really no Gospel at all. Evidently, some people are throwing you into confusion and are trying to pervert the

Gospel of Christ. But even if we or an angel from heaven should preach a Gospel other than the one we preached to you, let them be under God's curse!"

The Impact of Jesus' Ministry

During His ministry, Jesus served as a unifying force for the apostles and disciples. His teachings centered on seeking first the Kingdom of God and His righteousness. However, Jesus also caused division, separating true disciples from false ones. A notable example is found in **John 6:35–66**, where many disciples abandoned Him after He proclaimed:

"I am the bread of life. Whoever comes to Me will never go hungry, and whoever believes in Me will never be thirsty… Whoever eats My flesh and drinks My blood has eternal life, and I will raise them on the last day."

Many found this teaching difficult to accept and walked away. Yet, through such moments, Jesus brought clarity and unity among those who truly believed.

The First Major Division

The first significant division in the Jerusalem Church was caused by the Circumcision Party, who insisted that salvation required adherence to Jewish laws and traditions. This false Gospel undermined the sufficiency of Christ's sacrifice and created a barrier between Jewish and Gentile believers.

This issue not only divided the Jerusalem Church but also caused widespread rejection of the Gospel among Jews throughout the Middle East, Asia, and Greece. They could not accept a message that excluded circumcision and the Mosaic Law from salvation.

The Long-Term Consequences

The influence of the Circumcision Party persisted, eventually impacting the Church in Rome and shaping the doctrines of many churches over the centuries. This false Gospel diminished the power and authority of the Church, diverting attention from the freedom and victory available through Christ.

Examples of False Gospel Influence

Historical Persecution

Over centuries, churches that upheld the truth of the Gospel, free from legalistic additions, were persecuted by those aligned with the false Gospel.

- **Example 1:** Pentecostal missionaries evangelizing in Lagos, Nigeria, were arrested and imprisoned by members of the Church of Rome until their deaths.
- **Example 2:** In Britain, Catholics and Protestants alternately persecuted and executed one another for heresy, with religious and political power struggles defining much of the period from the reign of Henry VIII through the English Civil Wars.

Jesus said, *"You will know My followers by the love they have for one another."* (**John 13:35**)

Churches that persecute or kill fellow believers are operating under Satan's influence, not God's.

CHAPTER 4

The True Church in Antioch

The Church in Antioch serves as a powerful example of how a congregation can thrive when the Holy Spirit leads it. Unlike the Jerusalem Church, which struggled with legalism and the influence of the Circumcision Party, the Antioch Church embraced the Gospel's full message of freedom and grace.

A Spirit-Led Church

In Antioch, the Church operated with the fivefold ministry as described in **Ephesians 4:11**—apostles, prophets, evangelists, pastors, and teachers. The meetings were not bound by rigid structures but were instead guided by the Holy Spirit. Services often lasted late into the night or even into the next day as the Spirit moved freely among the congregation.

The manifestations of the Spirit's presence were evident:

- **Healing**
- **Deliverance**
- **Miracles**
- **Prophecies**
- **Words of knowledge**

It was here, under the Holy Spirit's direction, that the leaders of the Church prayed and laid their hands on Paul and Barnabas, sending them out as missionaries. The power of their ministry was confirmed by the signs and wonders that followed.

CHARACTERISTICS OF THE ANTIOCH CHURCH

1. **Unity of Faith**
   The members of the Church were unified in their faith in Christ, speaking the truth in love and growing in spiritual maturity.

2. **Spirit-Led Leadership**
   The leaders were appointed and anointed by God, confirmed by their ability to hear the Holy Spirit and perform signs and wonders.

3. **Purpose-Driven Ministry**
   The Church's goal was to equip the saints for ministry, build up the body of Christ, and bring believers into spiritual maturity.

4 **Freedom in Worship**
   Meetings allowed every member to contribute, emphasizing that all believers have a role in ministry.

This Spirit-led approach enabled the Antioch Church to thrive, standing in contrast to the challenges faced by the Jerusalem Church.

SATAN'S ATTACK ON ANTIOCH

Satan, seeing the success of the Antioch Church, attempted to corrupt it by sending members of the Circumcision Party. These individuals insisted that Gentile believers must be circumcised and obey the Law of Moses to be saved.

Paul fiercely opposed this attack. He convened a meeting with the apostles and elders in Jerusalem, where the Church ultimately sided with Paul, affirming that salvation comes through faith in Christ alone. A letter was sent back to Antioch, clarifying that Gentile believers were not bound by Jewish law.

However, Satan continued to target the Antioch-founded churches in Asia and Greece. His strategy included:

1. **False Apostles**
   Certain leaders in these churches refused to allow Paul's followers to speak, creating division and suppressing the truth.

2. **Loss of First Love**
   Some churches grew complacent, abandoning their original devotion to Christ.

3. **Compromise**
   Others adopted sinful practices, such as the deeds of the Nicolaitans or the doctrine of Balaam, which led to sexual immorality and idolatry.

4. **Spiritual Deadness**
   Some churches became spiritually lifeless, lacking the fruits of healing, miracles, or deliverance.

5. **Lukewarm Faith**
   Wealth and self-sufficiency caused others to become lukewarm, neither hot nor cold in their devotion to God.

These challenges are outlined in Paul's letters and the messages to the seven churches in Revelation.

The Legacy of Antioch

The Church in Antioch serves as a reminder of what the Church can achieve when it remains faithful to the Holy Spirit. The fivefold ministry, spiritual gifts, and active participation of all believers are hallmarks of a thriving congregation.

The purpose of these elements is clear, as outlined in **Ephesians 4:11–16:**

- To equip the saints for ministry
- To build up the body of Christ
- To bring unity in faith and knowledge of the Son of God
- To help believers reach spiritual maturity
- To prevent them from being swayed by false doctrines or deceitful schemes

Through these practices, the Church grows in love and truth, with every member contributing to the body's overall health and mission.

Conclusion

The Antioch Church stands as a model for modern congregations. Its Spirit-led structure, freedom in worship, and commitment to equipping believers demonstrate what is possible when the Holy Spirit is given full authority. Despite Satan's attempts to corrupt and divide, the Antioch Church remained faithful to the true Gospel, providing a powerful contrast to the legalism and compromise that plagued other churches.

CHAPTER 5

The Current Church

The state of many contemporary churches is deeply concerning. While some remain vibrant and Spirit-filled, many others have lost their purpose, power, and influence. These churches are no longer *"the salt of the earth"* or *"the light of the world"* as Jesus intended (**Matthew 5:13–16**). Instead, they have become ineffectual, offering little more than routine gatherings or social functions.

The general public often perceives the Church as powerless, ineffective, and irrelevant, apart from its charitable activities. Many churches fail to demonstrate the supernatural power of God—they do not heal the sick, cast out demons, or raise the dead. They lack evidence of the Kingdom of God at work.

The Greatest Challenge: Division and Doctrine

One of Satan's most effective strategies for destroying the Church today is division, often fueled by doctrinal disputes. The danger is so significant that I have dedicated an entire chapter (Chapter 12) to this issue.

Key Problems in the Current Church

1. **Rooted in the Roman Model**
   Many modern churches are based on the structure of the first Church in Rome rather than the Spirit-led model of Antioch.

2. **Preaching a False Gospel**
   Numerous churches teach doctrines that deviate from the simplicity and power of the Gospel as outlined in the New Testament (see the book of Galatians).

3. **Legalism and Tradition**
   Much of the doctrine in mainline and Pentecostal churches is rooted in the traditions of the Jewish Temple priests, incorporating rules and rituals not found in the New Testament.

4. **Lack of Spiritual Leadership**
   Many priests and pastors are not led by the Holy Spirit. They cannot hear God's voice or discern His leading.

5. **Superficial Faith**
   A significant number of clergy and congregants cannot confidently declare Jesus as their Lord and Savior.

6. **Absence of Relationship**
   Many leaders lack a personal relationship with Jesus and have not experienced God's love in a transformative way.

7. **Suppression of Authority**
   Churches often discourage believers from knowing or exercising their authority in Christ.

8. **Neglect of Spiritual Power**
   Few churches pray for healing, miracles, or deliverance with genuine faith and power.

9. **Clerical Hierarchies**
   Many church leaders see themselves as superior to the laity, reserving spiritual functions for ordained clergy.

10. **Rituals over Relationship**
    Some churches emphasize rituals, such as communion and confession, over fostering a personal relationship with God.

11. **Resistance to the Holy Spirit**
    Many congregations actively or passively block the Holy Spirit from ministering in their services.

12 **Reluctance to Evangelize**
   Some churches avoid outreach, particularly to marginalized groups, such as the homeless or those struggling with addiction.

13 Aging Congregations
Many churches are dying due to aging memberships, with little effort to attract or disciple younger generations.

14. Rejection of Apostolic Structure
Apostles, prophets, evangelists, pastors, and teachers—the fivefold ministry given by God—are often excluded from leadership structures.

15. Sectarianism
Some churches still harbor hostility toward other denominations, perpetuating division and hatred instead of unity and love.

These issues are not limited to a specific denomination but are widespread across mainline, evangelical, and Pentecostal churches.

HISTORICAL INFLUENCE

Many modern churches trace their roots back to the Church in Rome, which inherited elements of the Jewish Temple system. Over time, this structure emphasized hierarchy, rituals, and tradition, often at the expense of spiritual freedom and power.

The Church in Antioch, in contrast, operated under the guidance of the Holy Spirit. Unfortunately, Antioch-inspired churches were largely wiped out by Roman-aligned churches, which persecuted Spirit-led believers and destroyed congregations that did not conform to their doctrines.

Even today, churches that model themselves on the Roman system often suppress the move of the Holy Spirit, focusing instead on formalized ceremonies and clerical authority.

EXAMPLES OF MODERN FAILINGS

1. **A Divided Focus:** In one church, a pastor used his pulpit to discuss a sports event, the AFL finals, during the service. Immediately, the sound

system and projector failed, delaying the service for over half an hour. It seemed as though God was sending a message: *"You shall have no other gods before Me."*

2. **Discouraging Leadership:** At another church, I observed a young teenager leave the congregation, likely due to a lack of encouragement or meaningful engagement. Despite my repeated requests to hold ministry meetings in the church hall, the pastor denied me. Over time, many members of the parish council, frustrated by the pastor's resistance, resigned and left the church.

A Call to Return to the True Church

The current state of the Church calls for reflection and repentance. It is time to return to the principles of the Antioch Church—a Spirit-led model where all believers are empowered to fulfill their God-given roles.

As Jesus said:

"You will receive power when the Holy Spirit comes on you; and you will be My witnesses in Jerusalem, and in all Judea and Samaria, and to the ends of the earth." **Acts 1:8**

The Church must rediscover this power and embrace its true calling to advance the Kingdom of God, heal the broken, and proclaim the Gospel with boldness and authority.

CHAPTER 6

The True Gospel

The true Gospel is simple yet profound. It is the message of salvation through Jesus Christ, offered freely to all who believe. At its core, the Gospel is about restoring humanity's relationship with God through faith, not works, and about walking in the fullness of the victory Jesus secured on the Cross.

THE CORE MESSAGE OF THE TRUE GOSPEL

1. **Salvation by Grace Through Faith**
   Salvation cannot be earned; it is a gift from God. Paul states in **Ephesians 2:8–9:**

> *"For it is by grace you have been saved, through faith—and this is not from yourselves, it is the gift of God—not by works, so that no one can boast."*

The Cross was sufficient. Jesus paid the full price for our sins, and there is nothing we can add to His sacrifice.

2. **Freedom from the Law**
   The Law of Moses was a shadow of what was to come in Christ. Jesus fulfilled the Law, setting believers free from its demands and penalties. **Galatians 3:13** declares:

   > *"Christ redeemed us from the curse of the law by becoming a curse for us."*

3. **Empowerment Through the Holy Spirit**
   The Gospel is not just about salvation but also about transformation. When we receive the Holy Spirit, we are empowered to live victorious lives, as Jesus promised:

"You will receive power when the Holy Spirit comes on you." **Acts 1:8**

4. **Authority in Christ**
   Believers are given authority over the enemy and the power to advance the Kingdom of God. Jesus said:

   "Very truly I tell you, whoever believes in Me will do the works I have been doing, and they will do even greater things than these." **John 14:12**

5. **A Personal Relationship with Jesus**
   The essence of the Gospel is intimacy with God. Jesus Himself said:

   "I am the way and the truth and the life. No one comes to the Father except through Me." **John 14:6**

   The Gospel is not about religious rituals or intermediaries but about knowing Jesus personally.

Characteristics of a Gospel-Centered Life

When a believer understands and embraces the true Gospel, their life reflects the following characteristics:

- **Bold Faith**—trusting in God's promises and stepping out in obedience.
- **Spiritual Power**—demonstrating the Kingdom of God through signs, wonders, and miracles.
- **Love and Unity**—living in harmony with others, marked by selfless love.
- **Fruitfulness**—producing the fruit of the Spirit—love, joy, peace, patience, kindness, goodness, faithfulness, gentleness, and self-control **(Galatians 5:22–23)**.
- **Holiness**—walking in the righteousness of Christ, empowered by the Holy Spirit to resist sin.

THE GOSPEL IN ACTION

The early Church exemplified the true Gospel. In Acts, we see believers:

- Healing the sick.
- Casting out demons.
- Raising the dead.
- Preaching boldly, even in the face of persecution.

Their faith was not passive; it was alive, active, and transformative. The same Gospel is available to us today.

CONCLUSION

The true Gospel is the good news of Jesus Christ—His death, resurrection, and the outpouring of the Holy Spirit. It is a message of freedom, power, and intimacy with God. To embrace the true Gospel is to walk in the fullness of all that Jesus accomplished on the Cross, living as His witnesses, and advancing His Kingdom on earth.

CHAPTER 7

The False Gospel

A false Gospel is any message that distorts, diminishes, or adds to the truth of the Gospel of Jesus Christ. It misrepresents God's Word, leading believers away from the simplicity and power of salvation through faith in Christ.

CHARACTERISTICS OF A FALSE GOSPEL

1. **Adding to God's Word**
   A false Gospel often adds unnecessary rules or rituals, making salvation contingent on human effort rather than the finished work of Christ.

2. **Denying God's Promises**
   It questions or contradicts the authority of Scripture, implying that God's Word is not trustworthy or sufficient.

3. **Legalism**
   This involves teaching that salvation requires adherence to a set of rules or laws beyond faith in Christ. The early Church faced this issue with the Circumcision Party, which insisted on following the Law of Moses in addition to believing in Jesus.

4. **Diminishing Christ's Work**
   A false Gospel undermines the sufficiency of Jesus' sacrifice on the Cross, suggesting that His work was not enough.

5. **Restricting Authority**
   It often teaches that only certain individuals, such as priests or pastors, can exercise spiritual authority, denying the empowerment of all believers through the Holy Spirit.

6. **Promoting Fear and Unworthiness**
   False Gospels emphasize sin and human failure, causing believers to feel unworthy of God's grace and incapable of walking in their God-given authority.

EXAMPLES OF FALSE GOSPEL TEACHINGS

1. **"The Authority of Believers Has Ended."**
   This teaching claims that the authority Jesus gave His followers passed away with the first apostles, leaving modern believers powerless.

2. **"Only Priests or Pastors Have Authority."**
   This doctrine places spiritual authority solely in the hands of clergy, discouraging believers from stepping into their God-given roles.

3. **"You Are Just a Sinner."**
   While it is true that all have sinned, the false Gospel emphasizes this to the point of neglecting the transformative

power of salvation and the righteousness believers receive in Christ.

4. **"Works Are Necessary for Salvation."** By focusing on human effort, this teaching denies the grace of God and leads people into bondage rather than freedom.

THE DANGER OF FALSE GOSPELS

A false Gospel does more than mislead—it destroys lives and hinders the growth of the Church. Satan uses these distortions to keep Christians in a state of spiritual weakness, ensuring they never fully realize their identity in Christ or their authority over the enemy.

Galatians 1:6–9 offers a stern warning:

"I am astonished that you are so quickly deserting the one who called you to live in the grace of Christ and are turning to a different Gospel—which is really no Gospel at all. Evidently, some people are throwing you into confusion and are trying to pervert the Gospel of Christ. But even if we or an angel from

heaven should preach a Gospel other than the one we preached to you, let them be under God's curse!"

THE ROLE OF CHURCH LEADERSHIP IN FALSE GOSPELS

Unfortunately, church leaders often perpetuate false Gospels by:

- ᛋ Blocking the Holy Spirit from ministering freely.
- ᛋ Restricting the roles and authority of ordinary believers.
- ᛋ Clinging to human traditions and doctrines that conflict with Scripture.
- ᛋ Promoting a culture of fear, guilt, and control rather than love, grace, and freedom.

RECOGNIZING AND REJECTING A FALSE GOSPEL

To identify a false Gospel, we must ask these key questions:

1. Does this teaching align with Scripture?

2. Does it emphasize God's grace or human effort?
3. Does it empower believers to walk in their authority and relationship with Christ?
4. Does it produce the fruits of the Spirit?

If the answer to any of these questions is "no," then the teaching must be rejected.

Conclusion

The false Gospel is one of Satan's most effective tools for weakening the Church and deceiving believers. It robs the Church of its power, authority, and effectiveness. To combat this, we must remain rooted in the true Gospel—the message of grace, freedom, and empowerment through faith in Jesus Christ.

As Paul writes in **2 Corinthians 11:3–4:**

"But I am afraid that just as Eve was deceived by the serpent's cunning, your minds may somehow be led astray from your sincere and pure devotion to Christ. For if someone comes to you and preaches

a Jesus other than the Jesus we preached, or if you receive a different spirit from the Spirit you received, or a different Gospel from the one you accepted, you put up with it easily enough."

CHAPTER 8

God's Plan for the Church

God's plan for the Church is both profound and simple: to establish His Kingdom on earth, bringing salvation, healing, and restoration to all who believe. The Church is the body of Christ, called to reflect His glory and fulfill His mission.

THE PURPOSE OF THE CHURCH

1. **To Proclaim the Gospel**
   The Church's primary mission is to share the good news of Jesus Christ with the world. As Jesus instructed in **Matthew 28:19–20:**

> *"Therefore go and make disciples of all nations, baptizing them in the name of the Father and of the Son and of the Holy Spirit, and teaching them to obey everything I have commanded you."*

2. **To Demonstrate God's Power**
   The Church is not just a place of words but of action. Through the power of the Holy Spirit, the Church is called to heal the sick, cast out demons, and perform signs and wonders. Jesus declared in **Mark 16:17–18:**

> *"And these signs will accompany those who believe: In My name they will drive out demons; they will speak in new tongues; they will pick up snakes with their hands; and when they drink deadly poison, it will not hurt them at all; they will place their hands on sick people, and they will get well."*

3. **To Build Up Believers**
   The Church exists to disciple believers, helping them grow in faith,

maturity, and Christlikeness. Paul wrote in **Ephesians 4:12–13:**

"To equip His people for works of service, so that the body of Christ may be built up until we all reach unity in the faith and in the knowledge of the Son of God and become mature, attaining to the whole measure of the fullness of Christ."

4. **To Be a Light in the World**
   The Church is called to reflect God's love, mercy, and righteousness to a world in darkness. Jesus said in **Matthew 5:14–16:**

   "You are the light of the world. A town built on a hill cannot be hidden. Neither do people light a lamp and put it under a bowl. Instead, they put it on its stand, and it gives light to everyone in the house. In the same way, let your light shine before others, that they may see your good deeds and glorify your Father in heaven."

THE STRUCTURE OF THE CHURCH

God designed the Church to operate with a specific structure, empowering every believer to fulfill their role. This structure is outlined in **Ephesians 4:11:**

- ❧ **Apostles:** Sent ones who establish new works and provide oversight.
- ❧ **Prophets:** Those who hear and proclaim God's voice.
- ❧ **Evangelists:** Messengers who spread the Gospel.
- ❧ **Pastors:** Shepherds who care for and nurture the flock.
- ❧ **Teachers:** Instructors who impart God's truth and wisdom.

Each role is essential for the growth and health of the Church. Together, these ministries ensure that the Church remains unified, equipped, and effective.

EMPOWERING EVERY BELIEVER

God's plan for the Church is not limited to a select few. Every believer has a role to play in advancing His Kingdom. **1 Corinthians 12:27** says:

"Now you are the body of Christ, and each one of you is a part of it."

The gifts of the Holy Spirit—such as healing, prophecy, and discernment—are distributed to all believers as the Spirit wills. These gifts are not for personal gain but for the benefit of the entire body.

CHALLENGES TO GOD'S PLAN

Despite God's clear vision for the Church, many congregations struggle to fulfill their purpose due to:

1. **Lack of Unity:** Division within the Church weakens its witness and effectiveness.
2. **Resistance to the Holy Spirit:** Some churches hinder the Spirit's work, prioritizing human traditions over divine leading.
3. **Neglect of Spiritual Gifts:** Many believers are unaware of or do not use the gifts God has given them.
4. **Clericalism:** The elevation of clergy over laity creates a divide,

limiting the involvement of ordinary believers in ministry.

Returning to God's Design

To align with God's plan, the Church must:

- ♦ Embrace the leadership of the Holy Spirit in every aspect of ministry.
- ♦ Equip and empower all believers to use their gifts and fulfill their callings.
- ♦ Prioritize discipleship, ensuring that every member grows in faith and maturity.
- ♦ Cultivate unity, focusing on what unites us rather than what divides us.

Conclusion

God's plan for the Church is one of power, purpose, and participation. It is a vision of a united body, equipped by the Holy Spirit, boldly proclaiming the Gospel and demonstrating the Kingdom of God on earth. As Paul wrote in **Ephesians 3:10–11:**

"His intent was that now, through the Church, the manifold wisdom of God should be made

known to the rulers and authorities in the heavenly realms, according to His eternal purpose that He accomplished in Christ Jesus our Lord."

The Church is not just an institution—it is a movement, called to transform lives and nations for the glory of God.

CHAPTER 9

God-Appointed Church Structure

God's design for the Church is intentional and purposeful. The structure He established is meant to equip believers, unify the body of Christ, and advance His Kingdom on earth. The Church is not a human institution but a spiritual organism, and its structure must reflect the wisdom and will of God.

The Biblical Framework

The foundation of the Church's structure is outlined in **Ephesians 4:11–13,** which identifies five key ministries:

1. **Apostles:** Sent by God to establish and oversee new works; apostles provide spiritual guidance and ensure churches remain grounded in God's truth.
2. **Prophets:** Prophets discern and communicate God's will, bringing correction, encouragement, and direction to the Church.
3. **Evangelists:** Focused on spreading the Gospel; evangelists bring new believers into the body of Christ.
4. **Pastors:** Shepherds who care for the spiritual well-being of the congregation; pastors provide guidance, nurture, and support.
5. **Teachers:** Responsible for imparting sound doctrine; teachers equip believers with the knowledge needed to live according to God's Word.

These five offices work together to build up the Church and bring believers into spiritual maturity.

The Purpose of the Structure

The roles within God's Church are not about hierarchy or control but about service and empowerment. As Paul wrote:

Ephesians 4:12–13

"To equip His people for works of service, so that the body of Christ may be built up until we all reach unity in the faith and in the knowledge of the Son of God and become mature, attaining to the whole measure of the fullness of Christ."

The structure exists to:

- Equip believers for ministry
- Foster unity within the Church
- Encourage spiritual growth and maturity
- Protect against false teachings and divisive doctrines

Unity Through Diversity

The strength of the Church lies in its diversity. Each member of the body has a unique role to play, and no one part is more important than the other. Paul illustrates this beautifully in **1 Corinthians 12:14–20:**

"Even so the body is not made up of one part but of many. Now if the foot should say, 'Because I am not a hand, I do not belong to the body,' it would not for that reason stop being part of the body. And if the ear should say, 'Because I am not an eye, I do not belong to the body,' it would not for that reason stop being part of the body."

Each believer has been given spiritual gifts, and when these gifts are exercised collectively, the Church functions as a unified and effective body.

Challenges to God's Design

Over time, many churches have deviated from God's appointed structure, adopting man-made hierarchies and traditions that hinder the Church's mission. Common issues include:

1. **Clericalism:** Elevating clergy to an elite class, separating them from the laity.
2. **Resistance to Apostolic and Prophetic Roles:** Many churches ignore or reject the roles of apostles and prophets, limiting the Church's ability to grow and adapt.
3. **Overemphasis on Rituals:** Some congregations focus more on traditions and ceremonies than on empowering believers for ministry.
4. **Neglect of Spiritual Gifts:** Many churches fail to recognize or encourage the use of spiritual gifts, leaving believers unfulfilled and underutilized.

Returning to the Biblical Model

To realign with God's design, churches must:

- **Embrace the Fivefold Ministry:** All five roles—apostles, prophets, evangelists, pastors, and teachers—should operate in every church to ensure balance and effectiveness.
- **Empower Every Believer:** The Church must encourage and equip

all members to use their spiritual gifts and fulfill their God-given roles.
- **Cultivate Unity:** Churches should focus on building bridges rather than walls, emphasizing shared faith and purpose.
- **Be Led by the Holy Spirit:** Every decision and action must be guided by the Spirit, not by human traditions or personal preferences.

Conclusion

The structure of the Church is a reflection of God's wisdom and love. It is designed to empower believers, foster unity, and advance His Kingdom. When the Church operates according to His plan, it becomes a powerful force for transformation in the world.

As Paul wrote in **1 Corinthians 12:27–28:**

"Now you are the body of Christ, and each one of you is a part of it. And God has placed in the Church first of all apostles, second prophets, third teachers, then miracles, then gifts of healing, of helping, of guidance, and of different kinds of tongues."

The Church is at its best when every member fulfills their role, working together as one body to glorify God and bring His light to the world.

CHAPTER 10

Individual Christians

While the Church functions as the collective body of Christ, its effectiveness depends on the faith, obedience, and commitment of individual Christians. Each believer plays a vital role in fulfilling God's purposes, and the strength of the Church is directly tied to the spiritual health and maturity of its members.

THE IDENTITY OF A CHRISTIAN

1. **A Child of God:**
   Believers are adopted into God's family and are His sons and daughters.

> *"Yet to all who did receive Him, to those who believed in His name, He gave the right to become children of God."* **John 1:12**

2. **A New Creation:**
   Through faith in Jesus, Christians are transformed and made new.

   > *"Therefore, if anyone is in Christ, the new creation has come: The old has gone, the new is here!"* **2 Corinthians 5:17**

3. **A Temple of the Holy Spirit:**
   The Holy Spirit dwells within every believer, empowering them for a life of victory and service.

   > *"Do you not know that your bodies are temples of the Holy Spirit, who is in you, whom you have received from God? You are not your own; you were bought at a price. Therefore honor God with your bodies."* **1 Corinthians 6:19–20**

The Role of Individual Christians

1. **Living as Witnesses:**
   Christians are called to reflect Christ in their words, actions, and character.

   "Let your light shine before others, that they may see your good deeds and glorify your Father in heaven." **Matthew 5:16**

2. **Sharing the Gospel:**
   Every believer has a responsibility to share the good news of Jesus with others.

   "Go into all the world and preach the Gospel to all creation." **Mark 16:15**

3. **Walking in Authority:**
   Christians are given authority over the works of the enemy and are called to live boldly in faith. **Luke 10:19**:

   "I have given you authority to trample on snakes and scorpions and to overcome all the power of the enemy; nothing will harm you."

4. **Using Spiritual Gifts:**
   God has given every believer unique gifts to build up the Church and advance His Kingdom.
   1 Peter 4:10:

   "Each of you should use whatever gift you have received to serve others, as faithful stewards of God's grace in its various forms."

5. **Pursuing Holiness:**
   A Christian's life should reflect the character of Christ through obedience and spiritual growth.
   1 Peter 1:15–16:

   "But just as He who called you is holy, so be holy in all you do; for it is written: 'Be holy, because I am holy.'"

Challenges Faced by Individual Christians

1. **Spiritual Opposition**
   Satan seeks to discourage and distract believers, using fear, doubt, and temptation to weaken their faith.

2. **Complacency**
   Many Christians fall into routines, prioritizing comfort and convenience over spiritual growth and service.

3. **Isolation**
   Without a connection to a community of faith, individuals often struggle to maintain their spiritual health.

4. **Lack of Knowledge**
   Many Christians are unaware of their identity in Christ and the authority they possess, leaving them vulnerable to deception.

Overcoming Challenges

To remain strong and effective,
individual Christians must:

1. **Spend Time in God's Presence**
   Regular prayer and worship
   keep believers connected to God
   and aligned with His will.

2. **Study the Word of God**
   The Bible is the foundation of faith
   and the ultimate source of truth.

   Psalm 119:105:
   *"Your word is a lamp for my
   feet, a light on my path."*

3. **Cultivate a Relationship with the Holy Spirit**
   The Holy Spirit provides guidance,
   power, and comfort in every area of life.

4. **Engage in Fellowship**
   Being part of a community of faith
   strengthens and encourages believers.

Hebrews 10:25:
"Not giving up meeting together, as some are in the habit of doing, but encouraging one another—and all the more as you see the Day approaching."

5. **Serve Faithfully**
   Christians grow by serving others and stepping out in faith to use their God-given gifts.

Conclusion

The success of the Church depends on the commitment and spiritual health of individual Christians. As each believer embraces their identity, authority, and purpose in Christ, the Church becomes a powerful force for transformation in the world.

Philippians 2:13:

"For it is God who works in you to will and to act in order to fulfill His good purpose."

Each Christian has a vital role to play in advancing God's Kingdom. Together, we form the body of Christ, called to bring light, hope, and salvation to a broken world.

CHAPTER 11

People Appointed by God

Throughout history, God has chosen and appointed individuals to fulfill His purposes. These people are called not because of their qualifications but because of their willingness to submit to His will and obey His voice. God equips those He calls, empowering them with the Holy Spirit to accomplish what He has planned.

Characteristics of God-Appointed Individuals

1. **Called by God**
   God's appointment is not based on human standards but on His divine purpose.

   "Before I formed you in the womb I knew you, before you were born I set you apart; I appointed you as a prophet to the nations." **Jeremiah 1:5**

2. **Empowered by the Holy Spirit**
   Those appointed by God are equipped with spiritual gifts and power to carry out their mission.

   "But you will receive power when the Holy Spirit comes on you; and you will be My witnesses in Jerusalem, and in all Judea and Samaria, and to the ends of the earth." **Acts 1:8**

3. **Marked by Obedience**

   God-appointed individuals prioritize His will above their own, trusting Him even when the task seems impossible. *"Then I heard the voice of the Lord saying, 'Whom shall I send? And who will go for us?' And I said, 'Here am I. Send me!'"* **Isaiah 6:8**

4. **Demonstrate Spiritual Fruit**

   The evidence of God's appointment is seen in the fruit of their ministry—lives transformed, miracles performed, and the Gospel advanced. *"Thus, by their fruit you will recognize them."* **Matthew 7:20**

Examples of God-appointed People in Scripture

1. **Moses**

   God called Moses to lead the Israelites out of slavery in Egypt. Despite his initial reluctance, Moses obeyed, and God performed miracles through him, including parting the Red Sea.

2. **David**
   Chosen as king while still a shepherd boy, God anointed David to lead Israel. His heart for God and his reliance on Him set him apart as a man after God's own heart.

3 **The Prophets**
   Prophets like Elijah, Isaiah, and Jeremiah were appointed to speak God's truth, often in the face of opposition. They fulfilled their missions by relying on God's strength and guidance.

4. **The Apostles**
   Jesus personally chose the apostles to carry on His work after His resurrection. Despite their flaws and weaknesses, the Holy Spirit empowered them to spread the Gospel to the ends of the earth.

How to Recognize Someone Appointed by God

1. **They Walk in Authority**
   God-appointed individuals operate with a clear sense of purpose and divine authority.

> *"When Jesus had called the Twelve together, He gave them power and authority to drive out all demons and to cure diseases, and He sent them out to proclaim the Kingdom of God and to heal the sick."* **Luke 9:1–2**

2. Their Ministry is Confirmed by Signs and Wonders

God often confirms His call through miracles and spiritual fruit.

> *"Then the disciples went out and preached everywhere, and the Lord worked with them and confirmed His word by the signs that accompanied it."* **Mark 16:20**

3. They Face Opposition

Those appointed by God often face resistance, both from the enemy and from people who oppose their mission.

> *"If the world hates you, keep in mind that it hated Me first."* **John 15:18**

4. **They Point People to God, Not Themselves**
   A true servant of God gives glory to Him and leads others to a deeper relationship with Christ.

   "He must become greater; I must become less." **John 3:30**

MODERN-DAY APPOINTMENTS

God continues to appoint individuals today for specific tasks within His Kingdom. These roles may include:

- **Missionaries**—bringing the Gospel to unreached people groups.
- **Church Leaders**—shepherding God's people and equipping them for ministry.
- **Prophets**—delivering messages of encouragement, warning, or direction from God.
- **Evangelists**—proclaiming the Gospel with boldness and bringing others to faith in Christ.
- **Intercessors**—praying fervently for the Church, nations, and individuals.

Each role is vital, and God equips His chosen servants with the gifts and resources they need to succeed.

Responding to God's Call

When God calls, the appropriate response is one of humility, faith, and obedience. Like Isaiah, we must be willing to say, *"Here am I. Send me!"* This response often requires stepping out of our comfort zones and trusting God to provide the strength and wisdom needed.

2 Timothy 1:7 reminds us of this:

"For the Spirit God gave us does not make us timid, but gives us power, love, and self- discipline."

Conclusion

God-appointed individuals are essential to His plan for the Church and the world. Their willingness to obey His call and walk in His authority brings transformation, healing, and hope. As believers, we must support, encourage, and recognize those whom God has appointed while remaining open to His call in our own lives.

CHAPTER 12

Divisions in the Church

One of Satan's most effective strategies to weaken and destroy the Church is through division. When believers are divided, the Church loses its unity, power, and effectiveness. Jesus emphasized the importance of unity, praying in **John 17:21:**

"That all of them may be one, Father, just as You are in Me and I am in You. May they also be in Us so that the world may believe that You have sent Me."

Despite this call for unity, divisions have plagued the Church throughout history and continue to do so today.

The Root Causes of Division

1. **Doctrinal Disputes**
   Differences in interpretation of Scripture often lead to arguments and factions.

2. **Pride and Ego**
   Leaders and members sometimes place their own opinions, traditions, or preferences above God's Word, creating conflicts.

3. **Cultural and Ethnic Differences**
   The early Church struggled with tensions between Jewish and Gentile believers. Today, similar divisions exist based on race, culture, and socioeconomic status.

4. **Misuse of Authority**
   Church leaders who misuse their authority to control or suppress others often cause divisions.

5. **Resistance to the Holy Spirit**
   When churches reject the move of the Holy Spirit, they often alienate Spirit-led believers, creating a divide.

BIBLICAL EXAMPLES OF DIVISION

1. **The Early Church in Corinth**
   Paul addressed divisions in the Corinthian Church, where believers aligned themselves with different leaders (Paul, Apollos, Cephas).

   "I appeal to you, brothers and sisters, in the name of our Lord Jesus Christ, that all of you agree with one another in what you say and that there be no divisions among you, but that you be perfectly united in mind and thought." **1 Corinthians 1:10–12**

2. **The Circumcision Party**
   In the Jerusalem Church, a group insisted that Gentile converts must be circumcised and follow the Law of Moses. This caused significant conflict until the apostles clarified that salvation comes through faith in Christ alone **(Acts 15)**.

3. **The Pharisees and Sadducees**
   Even before the Church was established, divisions among religious leaders

in Israel weakened their ability to recognize and receive the Messiah.

THE CONSEQUENCES OF DIVISION

1. **Weakening of the Church's Witness**
   Division undermines the Church's ability to reflect God's love and unity to the world.
   "By this everyone will know that you are My disciples, if you love one another." **John 13:35**

2. **Loss of Spiritual Power**
   A divided Church is unable to move in the full power of the Holy Spirit.

3. **Hindrance to the Great Commission**
   When churches are focused on internal conflicts, they neglect their mission to make disciples and spread the Gospel.

4. **Emotional and Spiritual Harm**
   Division often leads to hurt feelings, broken relationships, and disillusionment among believers.

Steps to Overcome Division

1. **Focus on Christ**
   Jesus is the head of the Church, and unity comes from aligning with Him.

   "And He is the head of the body, the Church; He is the beginning and the firstborn from among the dead, so that in everything He might have the supremacy." **Colossians 1:18**

2. **Seek Humility**
   Pride often fuels division. Believers must humble themselves, prioritize others, and seek reconciliation.

   "Do nothing out of selfish ambition or vain conceit. Rather, in humility value others above yourselves, not looking to your own interests but each of you to the interests of the others." **Philippians 2:3–4**

3. **Adopt a Kingdom Perspective**
   Instead of focusing on denominational differences, churches should

unite around the common goal
of advancing God's Kingdom.

4. Forgive and Reconcile

Forgiveness is essential for healing
and restoring relationships
within the Church.

"For if you forgive other people when they sin against you, your heavenly Father will also forgive you. But if you do not forgive others their sins, your Father will not forgive your sins." **Matthew 6:14–15**

5. Be Led by the Holy Spirit

Unity is a work of the Spirit, not human effort. Churches must allow the Holy Spirit to guide their actions and decisions.

"Make every effort to keep the unity of the Spirit through the bond of peace." **Ephesians 4:3**

The Power of Unity

When the Church operates in unity, it becomes a powerful force for God's Kingdom. The early Church in Acts demonstrates the blessings of unity.

Acts 2:46–47:

"Every day they continued to meet together in the temple courts. They broke bread in their homes and ate together with glad and sincere hearts, praising God and enjoying the favor of all the people. And the Lord added to their number daily those who were being saved."

Conclusion

Division is one of Satan's primary strategies to weaken the Church, but it can be overcome through humility, forgiveness, and a focus on Christ. As believers, we are called to work together as one body, united in purpose and love.

Psalm 133:1:

"How good and pleasant it is when God's people live together in unity!"

The world will know the power and truth of the Gospel when the Church stands united, reflecting the love and glory of God.

CHAPTER 13

Satan's Strategy Against the Church

Satan's ultimate goal is to destroy the Church, preventing it from fulfilling its mission to advance God's Kingdom. His strategies are subtle and effective, often targeting the Church from within. By distorting the truth, sowing division, and fostering complacency, Satan weakens the body of Christ, hindering its ability to reflect God's glory and power.

Satan's Tactics Against the Church

1. **Promoting False Gospels**
   Satan distorts the true Gospel, introducing teachings that add to, subtract from, or contradict God's Word. These false doctrines undermine the sufficiency of Christ's sacrifice and lead believers astray.

   "I am astonished that you are so quickly deserting the one who called you to live in the grace of Christ and are turning to a different Gospel—which is really no Gospel at all." **Galatians 1:6–7**

2. **Sowing Division**
   Division weakens the Church's unity and witness. Satan uses pride, doctrinal disputes, and personal conflicts to create factions within the body of Christ.

   "If a house is divided against itself, that house cannot stand." **Mark 3:25**

3. **Blocking the Move of the Holy Spirit**
   Many churches resist the Holy Spirit's work, relying on human traditions or intellect instead of allowing God's Spirit to lead. This limits the Church's power and effectiveness.

4. **Suppressing Spiritual Authority**
   By convincing believers that spiritual authority is reserved for clergy or that it no longer exists, Satan ensures Christians remain passive and powerless.

   "I have given you authority to trample on snakes and scorpions and to overcome all the power of the enemy." **Luke 10:19**

5. **Encouraging Complacency**
   Comfort and routine often replace passion and purpose. A complacent Church loses its urgency to evangelize, pray, and pursue holiness.

6. **Instilling Fear and Doubt**
   Fear of rejection, persecution, or failure prevents believers from stepping

out of faith. Doubt about God's promises and power undermines confidence in His Word.

HISTORICAL EXAMPLES OF SATAN'S STRATEGY

1. **The Fall of the First Church in Jerusalem**
   The introduction of legalism through the Circumcision Party created division and diluted the Gospel, leading to the Church's eventual decline.

2. **The Romanization of the Church**
   As the Church in Rome gained political power, it adopted hierarchical structures and traditions that deviated from the Spirit-led model of Antioch. Over time, the Church suppressed spiritual gifts and relied on rituals rather than the Holy Spirit.

3. **Persecution of Spirit-Led Believers**
   Throughout history, Spirit-led churches and individuals have been persecuted by institutionalized

religion, often accused of heresy for embracing the fullness of the Gospel.

Satan's Strategy Today

In the modern Church, Satan continues to use these tactics to hinder its mission:

1. **Denominational Conflicts**
   Differences in doctrine and practice often create unnecessary divisions, distracting believers from their common purpose.

2. **Resistance to Change**
   Many churches cling to traditions and resist new movements of the Holy Spirit, stifling growth and innovation.

3. **Focus on Entertainment over Discipleship**
   In some churches, the emphasis on attracting crowds through entertainment overshadows the need for spiritual depth and transformation.

4. **Moral Compromise**
   By normalizing sin and discouraging accountability, Satan weakens the Church's witness and holiness.

HOW TO RECOGNIZE AND RESIST SATAN'S STRATEGY

1. **Stand Firm in the Truth**
   Believers must ground themselves in Scripture to discern and reject false teachings.

   "Stand firm then, with the belt of truth buckled around your waist." **Ephesians 6:14**

2. **Cultivate Unity**
   Churches should focus on what unites them—faith in Christ—rather than what divides them.

   "Make every effort to keep the unity of the Spirit through the bond of peace." **Ephesians 4:3**

3. **Submit to the Holy Spirit**
   Allow the Holy Spirit to lead and empower every aspect of ministry, from worship to evangelism.

4. **Exercise Authority in Christ**
   Christians must understand and walk in the authority given to them by Jesus.

   "Submit yourselves, then, to God. Resist the devil, and he will flee from you." **James 4:7**

5. **Pray Without Ceasing**
   Persistent prayer strengthens believers and equips them to overcome spiritual opposition.

   "Pray continually." **1 Thessalonians 5:17**

6. **Encourage Holiness and Accountability**
   The Church must uphold God's standards and hold one another accountable in love.

   "Be holy, because I am holy." **1 Peter 1:16**

Conclusion

Satan's strategy against the Church is not new, but it is effective when believers are unaware or unprepared. By recognizing his tactics and standing firm in the truth, the Church can overcome his schemes and fulfill its mission.

As Paul reminds us in **2 Corinthians 2:11:**
"In order that Satan might not outwit us. For we are not unaware of his schemes."

The Church is called to be vigilant, united, and Spirit-led, shining as a beacon of hope and truth in a world desperate for God's light.

CHAPTER 14

Overcoming Satan's Strategy

The Church has the power to overcome Satan's strategies through the authority of Jesus Christ, the guidance of the Holy Spirit, and unwavering faith in God's Word. Satan's plans may be subtle and persistent, but they are no match for the Church that stands united and Spirit-filled.

STEPS TO OVERCOME SATAN'S STRATEGIES

1. **Stand on God's Word**
   Scripture is the ultimate weapon against Satan's lies and deceptions.

Believers must study, meditate on, and apply God's Word daily.

"For the word of God is alive and active. Sharper than any double-edged sword, it penetrates even to dividing soul and spirit, joints and marrow; it judges the thoughts and attitudes of the heart." **Hebrews 4:12**

2. **Pray Without Ceasing**
Persistent, Spirit-led prayer is essential for spiritual victory. Prayer connects us to God, strengthens our faith, and enables us to intercede for others.

"And pray in the Spirit on all occasions with all kinds of prayers and requests. With this in mind, be alert and always keep on praying for all the Lord's people." **Ephesians 6:18**

3. **Live in the Authority of Christ**
Believers have been given authority over the works of the enemy. By walking in this authority, they can resist Satan and advance God's Kingdom.

"I have given you authority to trample on snakes and scorpions and to overcome all the power of the enemy; nothing will harm you." **Luke 10:19**

4. **Be Led by the Holy Spirit**
   The Holy Spirit equips and empowers believers to discern Satan's tactics and respond with wisdom and power.

   "For those who are led by the Spirit of God are the children of God." **Romans 8:14**

5. **Cultivate Unity in the Church**
   Unity is essential for the Church to operate effectively. When believers focus on their shared faith in Christ, they become a powerful force against the enemy.

   "I in them and You in Me—so that they may be brought to complete unity. Then the world will know that You sent Me and have loved them even as You have loved Me." **John 17:23**

6. **Exercise Spiritual Gifts**
   Spiritual gifts, given by the Holy Spirit, are powerful tools for ministry and spiritual warfare. When used correctly, they build up the Church and defeat the enemy's plans.

   "Now to each one the manifestation of the Spirit is given for the common good." **1 Corinthians 12:7**

7. **Practice Forgiveness and Reconciliation**
   Unforgiveness and bitterness create openings for Satan to sow division and discord. By forgiving others and seeking reconciliation, believers close these doors.

   "Be kind and compassionate to one another, forgiving each other, just as in Christ God forgave you." **Ephesians 4:32**

8. **Live a Holy Life**
   A life of obedience and holiness protects believers from Satan's attacks and strengthens their witness to the world.

> *"Submit yourselves, then, to God. Resist the devil, and he will flee from you."* **James 4:7**

9. Encourage Accountability and Discipleship

Being part of a faith community provides strength, encouragement, and accountability. Discipleship helps believers grow in their faith and equips them to stand firm against the enemy.

THE POWER OF WORSHIP

Worship is a powerful weapon against Satan. When believers praise and glorify God, His presence fills their lives and drives out the enemy. Worship aligns hearts with God's will and shifts the focus from problems to His greatness.

2 Chronicles 20:21–22:

"After consulting the people, Jehoshaphat appointed men to sing to the Lord and to praise Him for the splendor of His holiness as they went out at the head of the army, saying: 'Give thanks to the Lord, for His love endures forever.' As they began to

sing and praise, the Lord set ambushes against the men of Ammon and Moab and Mount Seir who were invading Judah, and they were defeated."

Spiritual Armor

Paul emphasizes the importance of putting on the full armor of God to stand against Satan's schemes.

Ephesians 6:11–17:

"Put on the full armor of God, so that you can take your stand against the devil's schemes. For our struggle is not against flesh and blood, but against the rulers, against the authorities, against the powers of this dark world and against the spiritual forces of evil in the heavenly realms. Therefore put on the full armor of God, so that when the day of evil comes, you may be able to stand your ground, and after you have done everything, to stand. Stand firm then, with the belt of truth buckled around your waist, with the breastplate of righteousness in place, and with your feet fitted with the readiness that comes from the gospel of peace. In addition to all this, take up the shield of faith, with which you can extinguish all the flaming arrows of the evil one. Take the helmet of salvation and the sword of the Spirit, which is the word of God."

Conclusion

Satan's strategies are relentless, but the Church has been equipped with everything needed to overcome them. Through the Word of God, prayer, unity, and the power of the Holy Spirit, believers can stand firm and advance God's Kingdom.

Romans 8:37:

"No, in all these things we are more than conquerors through Him who loved us."

Victory belongs to the Church that remains faithful, Spirit-led, and united in purpose. Together, we can overcome the enemy and fulfill the mission God has entrusted to us.

CHAPTER 15

Spiritual Warfare

Spiritual warfare is the battle that takes place in the unseen realm between the forces of good and evil. Every believer is engaged in this conflict, whether they are aware of it or not. Understanding and actively participating in spiritual warfare is essential for living a victorious Christian life and advancing God's Kingdom.

The Reality of Spiritual Warfare

1. **The Enemy**
   Satan and his demons are the primary adversaries in this battle. Their mission is to steal, kill, and destroy (**John 10:10**).

2. **The Battlefield**
   Spiritual warfare takes place in the unseen, spiritual realm but manifests in the physical world through temptations, challenges, and opposition.

   "For our struggle is not against flesh and blood, but against the rulers, against the authorities, against the powers of this dark world and against the spiritual forces of evil in the heavenly realms." **Ephesians 6:12**

3. **The Stakes**
   The outcome of spiritual warfare affects the lives of individuals, the unity of the Church, and the advancement of God's Kingdom.

Weapons for Spiritual Warfare

1. **The Word of God (The Sword of the Spirit):** Scripture is the most powerful weapon against Satan's lies and schemes. Jesus used the Word of God to overcome temptation in the wilderness **(Matthew 4:1–11)**.

   "For the word of God is alive and active. Sharper than any double-edged sword, it penetrates even to dividing soul and spirit, joints and marrow; it judges the thoughts and attitudes of the heart." **Hebrews 4:12**

2. **Prayer**
   Prayer is both a weapon and a defense. It connects believers to God, aligns them with His will, and unleashes His power against the enemy.

   "The prayer of a righteous person is powerful and effective." **James 5:16**

3. **Faith (The Shield of Faith)**
   Faith extinguishes the flaming arrows of doubt, fear, and accusation that Satan hurls at believers.

   "In addition to all this, take up the shield of faith, with which you can extinguish all the flaming arrows of the evil one." **Ephesians 6:16**

4. **The Blood of Jesus**
   The blood of Christ is the foundation of victory in spiritual warfare. It overcomes the enemy and secures believers' authority in Christ.

   "They triumphed over him by the blood of the Lamb and by the word of their testimony; they did not love their lives so much as to shrink from death." **Revelation 12:11**

5. **Worship and Praise**
   Worship shifts the focus from problems to God's greatness, inviting His presence and power into the situation.

6. **Unity**
   A united Church is a powerful force against Satan's strategies. Division weakens the body of Christ, while unity strengthens it.

THE ARMOR OF GOD

Paul outlines the spiritual armor that every believer must put on to stand against the enemy.

Ephesians 6:13–17:

"Therefore put on the full armor of God, so that when the day of evil comes, you may be able to stand your ground, and after you have done everything, to stand. Stand firm then, with the belt of truth buckled around your waist, with the breastplate of righteousness in place, and with your feet fitted with the readiness that comes from the gospel of peace. In addition to all this, take up the shield of faith, with which you can extinguish all the flaming arrows of the evil one. Take the helmet of salvation and the sword of the Spirit, which is the word of God."

STRATEGIES FOR VICTORY

1. **Know Your Identity in Christ**
   Believers must understand their authority as children of God and co-heirs with Christ.

   "I have given you authority to trample on snakes and scorpions and to overcome all the power of the enemy; nothing will harm you." **Luke 10:19**

2. **Recognize the Enemy's Tactics**
   Satan uses deception, fear, and distraction to attack believers. Being aware of his schemes helps Christians resist them.

   "In order that Satan might not outwit us. For we are not unaware of his schemes." **2 Corinthians 2:11**

3. **Stay Spiritually Alert**
   Vigilance is essential in spiritual warfare. Believers must remain watchful and prayerful.

> *"Be alert and of sober mind. Your enemy the devil prowls around like a roaring lion looking for someone to devour."* **1 Peter 5:8**

4. Engage in Persistent Prayer
Prayer must be continual and Spirit-led to break strongholds and claim victory.

> *"Pray continually."* **1 Thessalonians 5:17**

5. Use Your Spiritual Gifts
The gifts of the Holy Spirit are given to equip believers for spiritual battles and ministry.

> *"Now to each one the manifestation of the Spirit is given for the common good."* **1 Corinthians 12:7**

The Role of the Church in Spiritual Warfare

The Church is not just a battleground but a force for advancing God's Kingdom. Together, believers are called to:

- **Pray and intercede for the world.**

- **Proclaim the Gospel with boldness.**
- **Stand against injustice and oppression.**
- **Support and encourage one another in faith.**

Conclusion

Spiritual warfare is a reality that every believer must face. However, through the power of God, the authority of Christ, and the guidance of the Holy Spirit, victory is assured.

Romans 8:37:

"No, in all these things we are more than conquerors through Him who loved us."

The battle belongs to the Lord, and those who trust in Him will overcome.

CHAPTER 16

The Final Victory

The story of humanity and the Church culminates in one undeniable truth: **Jesus Christ is victorious.** The final victory belongs to God, and this triumph will bring the ultimate defeat of Satan, sin, and death. This chapter explores the glorious future that awaits believers and the fulfillment of God's eternal plan.

THE PROMISE OF VICTORY

1. **Jesus Has Already Won**
   Through His death and resurrection, Jesus secured victory over Satan and the powers of darkness.

   "And having disarmed the powers and authorities, He made a public spectacle of them, triumphing over them by the cross." **Colossians 2:15**

2. **Satan's Defeat is Certain**
   Although Satan continues to oppose God's people, his ultimate destruction has been decreed.

   "And the devil, who deceived them, was thrown into the lake of burning sulfur, where the beast and the false prophet had been thrown. They will be tormented day and night for ever and ever." **Revelation 20:10**

3. **The New Heaven and New Earth**
   God will create a new heaven and a new earth, where righteousness

dwells, and His people will live in perfect harmony with Him forever.

"Then I saw 'a new heaven and a new earth,' for the first heaven and the first earth had passed away, and there was no longer any sea. I saw the Holy City, the new Jerusalem, coming down out of heaven from God, prepared as a bride beautifully dressed for her husband. And I heard a loud voice from the throne saying, 'Look! God's dwelling place is now among the people, and He will dwell with them. They will be His people, and God Himself will be with them and be their God.'" **Revelation 21:1–3**

The Nature of the Final Victory

1. **The Resurrection of the Dead**
   At the end of time, all the dead will be raised, and believers will receive glorified bodies.

   "For the trumpet will sound, the dead will be raised imperishable, and we will be changed. For the perishable must clothe

itself with the imperishable, and the mortal with immortality. When the perishable has been clothed with the imperishable, and the mortal with immortality, then the saying that is written will come true: 'Death has been swallowed up in victory.'" **1 Corinthians 15:52–54**

2. **The Final Judgment**

    All people will stand before God to be judged. Those whose names are written in the Lamb's Book of Life will enter eternal life, while those who rejected Christ will face eternal separation from God.

    "And I saw the dead, great and small, standing before the throne, and books were opened. Another book was opened, which is the book of life. The dead were judged according to what they had done as recorded in the books." **Revelation 20:12–15**

3. **The Eradication of Evil**

    Sin, suffering, and death will be eliminated forever.

> *"He will wipe every tear from their eyes. There will be no more death or mourning or crying or pain, for the old order of things has passed away."* **Revelation 21:4**

4. **Eternal Communion with God**
   Believers will dwell in the presence of God, experiencing His glory and love for eternity.

   > *"No longer will there be any curse. The throne of God and of the Lamb will be in the city, and His servants will serve Him. They will see His face, and His name will be on their foreheads."* **Revelation 22:3–4**

LIVING IN THE HOPE OF VICTORY

1. **Faith in God's Promises**
   Believers are called to trust in the certainty of God's victory, even when facing trials and opposition.

   > *"For our light and momentary troubles are achieving for us an eternal glory that far outweighs them all. So we fix our eyes not on what is seen, but*

on what is unseen, since what is seen is temporary, but what is unseen is eternal." **2 Corinthians 4:17–18**

2. **Perseverance in Trials**
Knowing the end of the story gives believers strength to endure hardships, secure in the knowledge that victory is assured.

"Blessed is the one who perseveres under trial because, having stood the test, that person will receive the crown of life that the Lord has promised to those who love Him." **James 1:12**

3. **Advancing God's Kingdom**
Until the final victory is realized, the Church is called to proclaim the Gospel, serve others, and stand against the forces of darkness.

"And this Gospel of the Kingdom will be preached in the whole world as a testimony to all nations, and then the end will come." **Matthew 24:14**

Conclusion

The final victory is not just a future event—it is a reality that shapes how believers live today. Jesus has already conquered sin, death, and Satan, and His triumph will be fully revealed at the end of time. Until that day, the Church must stand firm, united in purpose, and confident in the hope of eternal life.

Romans 16:20:

"The God of peace will soon crush Satan under your feet. The grace of our Lord Jesus be with you."

Victory belongs to the Lord, and His people will share in His glory forever.

ABOUT THE AUTHOR

Michael Shenton was brought up in Swansea, UK, in a council house estate. He originally joined the Welsh Church of England when he was 4 years old until he was approximately 14 years old.

Michael was in the Church Choir and a Server at Church Communion / Evensong for 4 years. He moved to Bunbury, WA, in 1987 and later became a member of the Anglican Church Healing Ministry Team run by Joe Hopkins. While in the ministry, Michael saw many healings and minor miracles during that time.

In 1999, God called Michael to start a Revival at St. Nicholas Church Australind, WA. He

received his Prophetic Office from Paul Cain
and his Apostolic Office from John Wimber.

Michael's ministry is like Paul to Timothy.
He prays for people to receive the gifts of the
Holy Spirit and then prays for their ministry
to be in God's providence continually. He
also trains and mentors the members and
supports them in their ministry's needs.

Michael is not and has never been interested in
the gains of his own ministry but is rather more
interested in supporting and uplifting others.

Michael's ministry is very simple—he listens
to the Holy Spirit and carries out whatever
the Holy Spirit enlightens him to do.

Personally, Michael had met Jesus several times,
not in a vision but face-to-face. Also, he had been
to Heaven approximately over 30 times. This
meeting with Jesus and being taken to Heaven is
available to anyone, same with John and Paul, who
met Jesus and were taken to Heaven, and Michael
does not see that he is any different from them.

Despite the rare opportunity of witnessing and feeling God, Michael still sees himself as no one special. He thinks anyone can do what he does if they have unwavering faith in God and a formidable relationship with Him.

Michael hopes that his experiences with God encourage you to never be afraid in seeking and creating your spiritual journey with Him.

www.ingramcontent.com/pod-product-compliance
Lightning Source LLC
Chambersburg PA
CBHW030526080526
44586CB00011B/337